The Truth, They Don't Want Us To Know.

I0438474

Who are they? And what don't they want us to know?

By Brother Anthony J F Mantova S.F.O.

Intentionally left blank.

Who are they? And what don't they want us to know?

This may very well be a short book, but the facts/truth are often short. It is the lies and false stories that are embellished beyond all recognition.

Well they are the Government and authorities of every country in the world/ on / off this planet!!

Firstly, regardless of who we are we are and what we or our ancestors have or have not done we are all human, so therefore all the same, all equal. So therefore how can and dare anyone claim to be above another or have more power or control than anybody else. They can't.

Secondly, we all say THE LAW! But what law, whose law? If as it is the law is made up by men/man and now days some women, is it actually the law? It is different in every country, some countries say innocent till proven guilty, other are opposite saying guilty till proven innocent, some ay any homosexuality is illegal, some just to gay, others to be lesbian.

Most countries have different legal ages of sexual consent. Like UK, 16, France, 15, Italy 14 Spain and Portugal 13. Whilst other have none but you must be married, and thus you can married in most Muslim Countries a young girl 5, 6 years or so.

Until everyone not each separate nation but the whole planet can agree THE LAW can we really claim to be a civilised people. By the time that happens, will it be too late? More importantly will we have need for such laws, seeing that we are all equal.

David Cameron was opposed to Juncker becoming next E.U. President, because he wants a tighter, more coherent Europe, then why Mr Cameron are you opposed? This is the begging of world unity and peace, that we all claim to want.

Now every Judge, Magistrate, Police Officer, Prison Officer and Politician, is only a human being, so why should we place so much faith and trust in them, and fear them, regardless of whether we have or have not in their eyes committed a crime. After all they are humans, and the tax payers pay their wages.

 They in turn pay taxes, and its those taxes that pay fr people to be arrested, taken to court, and put in prison, for X number of hours, days, weeks, years or life. Last I heard it was almost £160 to keep a person in jail, before the cost of food, water etc. That's UK do we know the cost in every other country?

Secondly religion, not only has the Christian religion, once only Catholic bee subdivided, it appears its true of every religion, hence terms like extremist, hardcore etc.

Now we know that the Muslim and Jewish faiths don't worship Christ, but by their own admission are aware and respect the Catholic/Christian faith, particularly the Blessed Virgin Mary, who was appeared to by the Angel Gabriel, the same angel who visited the prophet Mohamed.

But why then all the wars in the name of religion, Allah, Yahweh, Jehovah, GOD. The truth is if we strip every religion to its base elements 4 or 5 exist that are the same world over.

Belief, Faith, Peace, Respect and the greatest LOVE. For, our selves, each other and each others beliefs. This means that there is no right or wrong religion,

that as long as you believe is the real issue, now you might say, heathens, atheists, pagans. Well they all have a faith a belief, even if it is in believing, that there is no faith, therefore the believe in not believing..

Thirdly, The homosexual thing as many see it ,is actually as old as man/humanity itsself. In fact before we were human, the animal kingdom which created us with whatever help, has been and continues to be gay, bi, straight, so therefore it is nature, thus natural to be of any or all sexual persuasions.

It wen on for centuries, before we were told it is wrong etc, but now back to being accepted. The thing is when the men and young adults would go off hunting gathering for days, weeks even months, they must have had sexual urges and desire, as did the women, young ladies, and children who were left behind.

Therefore all of this is what makes us human, so let us embrace our differences, which unites us, fo without us and our differences we would not be here, and without us no world/planet/earth. As the custodians of this planet and its future, we need to stop saying my country, and start saying in unison my world, forget borders, passports, etc, because we own everything this planet is and has to offer.

So then, to save our money, lets get rid of the so called law and all the establishments they believe they have, as a) they belong to the taxpayer, and b) the taxpayer should decided where their money goes not them. The Pope, Queen, and every other member of this UK Royal family and every royal family, like everyone else is human, has no power or authority over another .

If you just take the time to look at the whole big picture and ask the relevant questions you'll see I am right. Our money in being wasted on thing and people it should not be spent on, yes health including ambulances services, education, fire services, are relevant the so called legal system is not.

This is our world lets embrace it and each other and all faiths, colours, languages sexualities etc.

Finally! This may be shocking , controversial and alarming, but however true, We have all heard about nasty Judges, Magistrates,

Police and Prison officers along with politicians being arrested and imprisoned for child sex assaults/abuse, Jimmy Saville knew some involved, and was not tackled to help maintain his silence.

The abuse happened then and is happening now. World over, but its not just child abuse, its rape, murder, torture, theft, fraud, tax evasion, drug tacking, making, selling, speeding, witness tampering, witness intimidation etc.

In fact if you can think of a crime, those meant to stop it, are committing it. And all in the name of the people, government, here in UK Our Queen, and the other Royal Families, Presidents,

Chancellors Prime Ministers etc around the world..

The tax payer is paying their wages, but shouldn't we have a right, in fact we do we should be telling them how we want our money spent, on what and where.

If the world stops paying taxes, until we get it to here it is needed, the so called powers that be will have to listen to us poor people. Poor, if we didn't waste money on useless taxes no one would be poor.

They do not have enough prisons now, and cannot build more if we stop payments, so they are screwed like the children they abuse. Also in the UK at least we have a law that says 18+ is an adult, however in jail, anyone up to 21 is a Y.O. Young Offender, how can this be as they are by law adults at 18? Is this some way of getting young people to abuse???

Mind you, despite being put in to prison which is an unlawful act breeching human rights on so mant levels, the prisoners are given jobs and or education, food and drink etc and its all paid for by the supposed law upholders.

EVEN THE WAGES FOR EMPLOYMENT AND EDUCATION.

So this is why after release many actively choose to commit crime to back, see their friends, cut down their own families bills etc, and who says crime doesn't pay. Trust me I know, I was set up on three occasions by nasty people.

The least mentioned the better, publicity was the real ideal goal, but even that backfired as everyone could see it.

So please, please, please people of the world unite, say enough is enough. We shall pay no more till our demands are met. Until the law is at least unified, and our taxes go to the right people.

Now I know you going to ask how can we stop them, why should we stop them, will we be arrested if we do and many more questions besides, the fact is we needed and must stop them.

Who do they think they are? Well clearly, they don't believe they are human, in fact they think their better than everyone else! They are not!! Did not Jesus say the master shall serve the servant, as the servant serves the master? So that is to say everyone equal. Even St Francis' prayers tells us to serve each other is better than to be served.

Yet we can only truly be united if we all, yes ALL!!! Come and work together as one planet not the individual pieces we are told we must be. Faith of every kind makes us human, yet to be worthy of the divine we must unite.

Yes there will be times we differ on many thing, but that also makes us human!!!

As I have Said, this is our planet, lets keep it that way. There can be no greater loss to the planet than another's life. No faith or law tells us to kill, so why do we. "Oh this is a holy War" "our law says its ok to kill to defend" is what we here.

Are you serious, that's a nasty excuse told by the nasty false powers that be. They Shall Be No More!!

The prayer of St. Francis

Lord, make me an instrument of your peace,
Where there is hatred, let me sow love;
where there is injury, pardon;
where there is doubt, faith;
where there is despair, hope;
where there is darkness, light;
where there is sadness, joy;

O Divine Master, grant that I may not so much
seek to be consoled as to console;
to be understood as to understand;

to be loved as to love.

For it is in giving that we receive;
it is in pardoning that we are pardoned;
and it is in dying that we are born to eternal
life.

St. Francis was born at Assisi in 1182. After a care free youth, he turned his back on inherited wealth and committed himself to God. Like many early saints, he lived a very simple life of poverty, and in so doing, gained a reputation of being the friend of animals. He established the rule of St Francis, which exists today as the Order of St. Francis, or the Franciscans.

He died in 1226, aged 44.
The prayer has many of the biblical truths of what it means to be a Christian - to seek to give, and in so doing, receive blessings; that the Lord's Prayer asks God to forgive us as we forgive, and that the goal of eternal life can only result from us putting to death our old sinful lives.

About the author!

Bother Anthony James Francis Mantova S.F.O. is a member of the Secular, Third, or Tertiary Order of St Francis of Assisi. The other abbreviations are T.O.F., O.F.S. and many more, if you wish to know more, about the order , St Francis of Assisi or any St or blessed from the life whether he or she be 1st, 2nd or 3rd order, then just search online.

Anthony was born in Liverpool, in 1977, never went to university but by no means un-educated. Has been an actor, writer, producer. He used to run a voluntary arts organisation etc. Be an extra on film and TV such as Hollyoaks Indecent Behaviour.

His original idea was to join the Friars Conventual, one of the three 1st order groups, but it never worked out and so joined the S.F.O. in August 2001.

He a great devotion and spirituality for all things Franciscan and is happy to spread devotion to the saint of nature. One can say that he is a naturist, though I think they mean naturalist.

Anthony also is living with / surviving MS (Multiple Sclerosis) And gets around by electric scooter, wheelchair and crutches. Has dyslexia and dyspraxia, yet is able to live as full and normal a life as can be expected.